Observe, admire, remember ...
Save the beauty for my children!

Photography, text, design
Bogdan KLADNIK

English version
Henrik CIGLIČ

German version
Wolfgang ZITTA

Italian version
SKRIVANEK d.o.o.

Technical setting
Sebastjan GORJAN

Published by
ZAKLAD, Ljubljana

Representative
Bogdan KLADNIK

For more information on our books write to:
Založba ZAKLAD, Čižmanova 6, 1211 Ljubljana, Slovenija,
call: +386 (0) 41 633 328
or visit: www.zaklad.si

Lithography
Camera, Ljubljana

Print and binding
Tiskarna knjigoveznica Radovljica

CIP - Kataložni zapis o publikaciji
Narodna in univerzitetna knjižnica, Ljubljana

908(497.4)(084.12)
77.047.1(497.4)

KLADNIK, Bogdan
  Bled & Bohinj : impressions / photography, [text] by Bogdan
Kladnik ; [English version Henrik Ciglič, Italian version Skrivanek,
German version Wolfgang Zitta]. - Ljubljana : Zaklad, 2005

ISBN 961-6266-20-9

220931328

View of Lake Bled from the Osojnica viewpoint *(page 4)*
Bohinj - The Alpine Oasis *(page 6)*

BLED AND BOHINJ

Imagine that you are the first human in the Earth's history that has just reached the viewing hillock Osojnica above Bled and laid eyes on the romantic little lake with an islet in the middle and the scenery of high mountains in the background. No hotels, no roads, no houses, not even the graceful little church and the prominent castle above the lake. Only forests, water and mountains – a pure, unspoiled landscape. You'd probably think that there is no nicer place in the entire world. And you'd be more or less right, for in spite of it all it is still a view that you'd find it difficult to find anywhere else on the planet.

Now let us return from these dreams to the present time, to the facts and descriptions relevant for the modern visitor.

At the foot of the Julian Alps lie the two best known Alpine lakes: the first is Lake Bled, from the 19th century onwards the most prominent tourist centre of Slovenia. The islet in the middle of the lake was frequented as early as in prehistory, while a millennium ago, on April 10th, 1004, the place Bled itself was mentioned for the first time, i.e. in the deed according to which the German Emperor Henry II donated it to Albuin, the Bishop of Brixen. Bled gained its international reputation mostly due to its sanatorium, founded by the Swiss hydropathist Arnold Rikli. The place, which was in the early 20th century the finest health resort in the Austrian empire, attracted numerous members of the European aristocratic elite. After World War II, one of the most beautiful protocolary residences of the former state stood here, and the beauties of Bled were enjoyed by most prominent people from all over the world. The town of Bled is situated on the fringe of Triglav National Park and is an ideal starting-point for the visit of its natural beauties, considering that many accessible and highly interesting places (Vintgar Gorge, Pokljuka Gorge, Pod Babjim zobom Cave, Lake Bohinj, Pokljuka Plateau) lie virtually in its immediate vicinity.

In winter, the islet and the castle are surrounded by fabulous landscape, ideal for walks around the lake covered with ice, for cross-country skiing, or trekking into the very heart of Triglav National Park. The best known cross-country skiing centre is Pokljuka, the karst plateau accessible both from Bled and Bohinj. It is situated at an altitude between 1200 and 1500 metres and considered a true paradise for cross-country skiers. Between the woods only some 28 km up the Sava Bohinjka Valley, we shall catch sight of the following remarkable feature of the Julian Alps – Lake Bohinj. It lies 525 m above the sea and is 4100 m long, 1200 m wide, and up to 45 m deep. With its surface area of 3.18 km² it is the largest permanent lake in Slovenia. During the winter it is almost invariably frozen over, while in the summer its upper layer warms up to 22º C, making it suitable for swimming and rowing. Into the lake flows, as its main surface affluent, the crystal-clear Savica, which finds its source in the waterfall in the extreme upper part of the basin. It is supplied by the waters of the Seven Triglav Lakes situated approximately a thousand metres above the lake.

The water comes boiling from a joint in the Komarča rockwall at an altitude of 836 m, then flows over the 38 m long slope, and finally tumbles almost perpendicularly 51 m deep. The Savica waterfall is certainly the best visited and most remarkable Slovene waterfall. The lake is also filled by several smaller springs on its northern side. Its waters finally leave it as the Sava Bohinjka river at the Church of St. John the Baptist.

The name Bohinj denotes not only the lake but the entire Alpine basin in the catchment of the Sava Bohinjka from the village of Soteska upwards. It is a good 20 km long and 5 km wide at the most. In its upper part it is a uniform Alpine basin, while in its middle part it splits into the parallel Lower and Upper Valleys. Bohinj is one of the most characteristic Alpine areas, where mountain pasturage has been particularly well developed in the past. If you drive to Bohinj, you can board the cable car, which will take you up to Mt. Vogel with its most unique ski slopes in the area of Triglav National Park and marvellous views of the Julian Alps, Lake Bohinj and the Karavanke mountain chain.

With its lake, Bohinj is by many people considered the most prominent, the most beautiful and the best naturally preserved part of the eastern Julian Alps. Let it stay such in the future as well!

Bled und Bohinj

Stellen Sie sich vor, Sie wären der erste Mensch, der in der Menschheitsgeschichte den Aussichtshügel Osojnica bei Bled je bestiegen und vor sich den romantischen See mit der kleinen Insel und der hohen Bergkulisse im Hintergrund erblickt hätte. Nirgends Hotels, Straßen, Häuser, auch das liebliche Kirchlein und die pittoreske Burg nicht. Nur Wälder, Wasser und Berge – pure, unberührte Naturlandschaft. Wahrscheinlich würden Sie denken, dass es auf der ganzen Welt keinen schöneren Ort gäbe. Und Sie würden nicht fehlgehen. Trotz allem ist dies noch heute ein Blick, der seinesgleichen sucht.

Doch kehren wir aus der Träumerei wieder zur Realität zurück, zu den Fakten und Darstellungen, die für den heutigen Besucher wichtig sind. Am Fuß der Julier liegen zwei sehr bekannte Alpenseen. Der erste ist der Bleder See, schon seit dem 19. Jahrhundert das typischste Fremdenverkehrszentrum Sloweniens. Die kleine Insel in der Seemitte wurde bereits in der Vorzeit besucht, und vor einem Jahrtausend, am 10. April 1004, wurde auch der Ort Bled erstmals erwähnt. Der deutsche Kaiser Heinrich II. schenkte ihn damals dem Brixener Bischof Albuin. Zum internationalen Renommee von Bled trug der Schweizer Hydropath Arnold Rikli mit der Anlage eines Klimakurorts viel bei. Der schon zu Beginn des 20. Jahrhunderts als schönster Kurort des damaligen Kaiserreichs bekannte Ort war ein Magnet der aristokratischen Elite Europas. Nach dem 2. Weltkrieg befand sich hier eine der schönsten Residenzen des damaligen Staates, und an den landschaftlichen Schönheiten von Bled erfreuten sich unzählige prominente Persönlichkeiten aus der ganzen Welt. Bled liegt am Rand des Nationalparks Triglav und ist ein idealer Ausgangspunkt zur Besichtigung seiner Naturschönheiten, liegen doch viele zugängliche und attraktive Sehenswürdigkeiten in unmittelbarer Nähe (Vintgar-Schlucht, Pokljuka-Schlucht, Höhle unter dem Babji zob, Bohinjer See, Pokljuka). Im Winter sind Insel und Burg von einer märchenhaften Landschaft umgeben, einem Paradies für Spaziergänge rund um den zugefrorenen See, für Langlauf oder Wanderungen ins Herzstück des Nationalparks. Das bekannteste Langlaufzentrum liegt auf der Pokljuka, einem waldreichen Karstplateau, das sowohl von Bled als vom Bohinj erreichbar ist. Es liegt 1200 bis 1500 Meter hoch und stellt ein Eldorado für Langläufer dar. Nur 28 Kilometer im Tal der Sava Bohinka aufwärts, mitten in den Bergen, liegt eine weitere Sehenswürdigkeit der Julischen Alpen, der Bohinjer See: 525 Meter über dem Meeresspiegel, 4100 Meter lang, 1200 Meter breit und bis 45 Meter tief. Mit einer Fläche von 3,18 Quadratkilometern ist er Sloweniens größter ständiger See. Im Winter friert er fast immer zu, und im Sommer erwärmt er sich bis 22 Grad und verlockt zum Baden und Rudern.

Den größten oberirdischen Zufluss bildet die klare Savica, die in einem mächtigen Wasserfall am obersten Ende des Talkessels entspringt. Sie wird von den etwa 1000 Meter höher liegenden Triglaver Seen gespeist. Das Wasser tritt in einer Höhe von 836 Metern aus einer Verwerfung in der Komarča-Wand hervor, fließt zunächst über eine 38 Meter lange schräge Stufe und stürzt dann 51 Meter fast senkrecht in die Tiefe.

Der Savica-Fall ist sicher der attraktivste und am häufigsten besuchte Wasserfall Sloweniens. Der See wird noch von mehreren kleineren Quellen auf der Nordseite gespeist, dann verlässt die Savica als Sava Bohinjka den See unter der Brücke bei der Johanneskirche.

Mit Bohinj wird nicht nur der See, sondern das gesamte Alpenbecken im Quellgebiet der Sava Bohinjka von der Siedlung Soteska aufwärts bezeichnet. Es ist rund 20 Kilometer lang und höchstens 5 Kilometer breit, der obere Abschnitt bildet ein geschlossenes Seebecken, während sich der mittlere in das parallel verlaufende Untere und Obere Tal gabelt.

Der Bohinj ist eine der typischsten Alpenlandschaften Sloweniens, in der sich die Almwirtschaft besonders stark entwickelte. Wenn man auf dem Weg zum Bohinj ist, kann man mit der Seilbahn auf den Vogel fahren, wo ein einzigartiges Skigebiet im Nationalpark Triglav mit prachtvollem Ausblick auf die Julier, den Bohinjer See und die Karawanken liegt.

Der Bohinj stellt mit seinem See für viele Besucher die großartigste, schönste und intakteste Naturlandschaft der östlichen Julier dar. Er soll auch so bleiben!

BLED E BOHINJ

Provate ad immaginare di essere il primo uomo della storia slovena a mettere piede sulla cima del colle Osojnica sopra Bled; di fronte a voi s'aprirebbe l'incredibile vista sul romantico laghetto, con l'isoletta in mezzo, e dietro lo sfondo delle alte montagne. Nessun albergo, niente strade o case, nemmeno la graziosa chiesetta o il famoso castello. Solamente boschi, acqua e monti – un paesaggio pulito, incontaminato. Pensereste che al mondo non ci sia posto più bello. E non sbagliereste. Nonostante tutti i cambiamenti, il panorama, ancora oggi, sembra non conoscere uguali. Usciamo ora dai sogni per ritornare alla realtà, ai fatti e ai dati che interessano al visitatore di oggi.

Ai piedi delle Alpi Giulie sono situati i due laghi alpini più famosi: il primo è il lago di Bled, rinomato centro turistico sloveno già a partire dal IX secolo. L'isoletta in mezzo al lago era meta di visitatori già migliaia di anni fa, nel periodo preistorico. Il toponimo di Bled viene menzionato per la prima volta il 10 aprile 1004, quando l'imperatore tedesco Enrico II donò la zona al vescovo Alboino di Bressanone. Bled cominciò a godere di fama mondiale grazie al medico idropatico svizzero Arnold Rikli che vi fondò un centro di cura climatico. Tale centro, considerato all'inizio del XX secolo il più bello di tutto l'Impero, attirò numerosi rappresentanti dell'elite aristocratica europea. Dopo la seconda guerra mondiale, Bled è stata una tra le più belle residenze protocollari dello stato di allora. Delle bellezze del luogo hanno goduto personaggi importanti venuti da tutto il mondo. La città di Bled è situata ai margini del Parco Nazionale del Triglav ed è il punto di partenza ideale per visitare le sue bellezze naturali, visto che, nelle sue immediate vicinanze, si trovano varie mete facilmente raggiungibili (la Gola del Vintgar, la Gola del Pokljuka, la grotta 'Pod Babjim Zobom', il Lago di Bohinj e il Pokljuka). Nella stagione invernale, l'isola e il castello assumono sembianze da favola, diventando lo scenario ideale per passeggiate attorno al lago di color verde ghiaccio, per lo sci da fondo o per passeggiate nel cuore del Parco Nazionale del Triglav. Il centro più conosciuto per lo sci da fondo è il boscoso altopiano carsico del Pokljuka, che si può raggiungere sia da Bled che da Bohinj. Ad un'altitudine compresa tra i 1200 e i 1500 metri, è un vero e proprio paradiso per i fondisti.

Risalendo di 28 km la vallata della Sava Bohinjka, si scorge, circondata dai monti, un'altra perla delle Alpi Giulie – il lago di Bohinj. A 525 m sul livello del mare, il lago è lungo 4100 m, largo 1200 m e profondo fino a 45 m. Con un'area di 3,18 km², è il più grande lago perenne sloveno. Nella stagione invernale è quasi prevalentemente ghiacciato, mentre d'estate la sua superficie raggiunge i 22° C, rendendolo così adatto alla balneazione e al canottaggio. Affluente principale del lago è il limpido fiume Savica che sgorga dalla cascata situata sulla parte più elevata del bacino. Il fiume è alimentato dalle acque dei Sette Laghi del Triglav, a circa mille metri più in alto. L'acqua sgorga da un'apertura della parete Komarče a 836 metri d'altezza, scorre diagonalmente per 38 m per poi cadere quasi a 51 m di profondità. La cascata Savica è indubbiamente la più conosciuta e visitata della Slovenia. Il lago è alimentato da numerose piccole sorgenti situate nella sua parte settentrionale; dal lago, l'acqua scorre poi prendendo il nome di Sava Bohinjka, passando sotto il ponte vicino alla chiesa di San Giovanni Battista.

Col nome Bohinj non si indicano solamente i laghi, bensì l'intero bacino alpino del tratto superiore della Sava Bohinjka, a partire dalla Gola. La Gola è lunga più di 20 km, con una larghezza massima di 5 km; la parte superiore comprende un unico bacino di laghi, quella centrale è suddivisa invece tra le due vallate parallele, la Valle Inferiore e quella Superiore. Bohinj rappresenta una delle regioni alpine più caratteristiche della Slovenia, nella quale sono notevolmente diffusi i pascoli alpini. Se vi recate a Bohinj, fatevi trasportare dalla funivia sul Vogel, straordinario campo da sci nel territorio del Parco Nazionale del Triglav, con un'incredibile vista sulle Alpi Giulie, sul Lago di Bohinj e sulle Caravanche.

Bohinj, insieme al suo lago, è da molti considerata la zona più rinomata, più bella e dalla natura più incontaminata delle Alpi Giulie Orientali. Speriamo che rimanga sempre così!

Bled Castle with Mt. Triglav (2864 m) in the background

View of Lake Bled from the Osojnica viewpoint in summer

Bled Islet with St. Mary's Assumption Church in summer

Bled Islet with St. Mary's Assumption Church in winter

Villa Prešeren

Lake Bled as seen from Bled Castle

View of Bled Castle from the town

Pokljuka Gorge

Vintgar Gorge

In the Vintgar Gorge

Lake Bled as seen from a hot air balloon

Bled Islet as seen from a boat

Magnificent views of the Gorenjska plain from Bled Castle *(facing page)*

View of Lake Bled from its southern shore
Church of St. Martin *(facing page)*

Bled - "pletna" boats

Bled Islet from a helicopter

Bled Islet and Castle, as seen from the southern shore of the lake

Zajamniki mountain pasture (1257 m) on the Pokljuka Plateau

Lake Bohinj in winter

Double hayrack at Studor

Church of Holy Spirit

The winter fairytale

The Sava Bohinjka river

Srednja vas
Church of St. John and the nearby stone bridge *(facing page)*

Lake Bohinj

Stara Fužina

Lake Bohinj, ideal for rowing fans

The Sava Bohinjka river

The source of Kropa (at different water-levels)

The Govic waterfall

The Savica waterfall

Studor, a picturesque Bohinj village

Double hayracks toplars at Studor

Climbing in the vicinity of Bellevue Hotel
Vogel ski area *(facing page)*

The Ribnica waterfall / The Peračica waterfall

The Mostnica waterfall / The Suha waterfall

Vodični vrh mountain pasture (1500 m)

Vodični vrh mountain pasture (1500 m) / Planina Viševnik mountain pasture (1615 m); *above,*
Planina pri jezeru mountain pasture (1453 m)

The Mostnica river in the Voje Valley

"Slonček" (Elephant Calf) in the Mostnica Gorge

The Mostnica Gorge

The Ribnica Gorge

The Grmečica Gorge

Mt. Ogradi (2087 m)

Planina v Lazu mountain pasture (1560 m)

Under Ogradi

Vodnik Chalet and Velo polje

Planika Chalet below Mt. Triglav

Double Lake
Valley of the Seven Triglav Lakes *(facing page)*

BOGDAN KLADNIK, born 1960 in Ljubljana. He is publishing his photographs and articles in the magazines Stern, Bell'Europa, Tuttoturismo, Berge, National Geographic Junior, National Geographic Adventure and Merian.

He is the author of about 100 picture post-cards, more than 80 calendars and some multimedia productions, which he has shown both at home and abroad (Belgium, Italy, Germany, Austria, France).

He has also prepared five exhibitions: one each in Novo mesto and Ljubljana, and three in France, where he was also a member of the jury set up for the speleology festivals. The only competition, at which he has participated in his entire life, was held in France: this was the Seventh Multimedia Festival on the subject of mountaineering in Briançon, 1993, where he was awarded first and second prizes, and the overall Grand Prix de Briançon for his multimedia exhibits "Eternal Cycle" and "Terra Mystica."

Above all he is the author and publisher of 38 photo-monographs about the Slovene natural and cultural heritage:
Terra Mystica (1991), Brdo, Strmol, Snežnik (1993), Soča (1994), Ljubljana (1994), Idrijski rudnik (1995), Portret Slovenije (1995), Večni krog (1995), Ljubljana (1996), Slovenija (1996), Soča (1997), Slovenija (1997), Novi portret Slovenije (1998), Okus teme (1998), Ljubljana (1999), Soča (1999), Gorenjska (1999), Vipavska dolina (1999), Slovenski mostovi I. del (2000), Portret Slovenije (2001), Soča (2001), Bled (2002), Slovenski mostovi II. del (2002), Slovenija brez meja (2003), Portret Slovenije (2003), Jame Slovenije (2003), Gore Slovenije (2003), Outdoor Slovenia (2005), Slovenija impressions (2005), Karst & Coast impressions (2005)...

"Bogdan Kladnik is not only an expert on natural beauties of Slovenia, its historical, artistic and ethnographic particularities and pearls; he belongs to the generation of the curious, of the photographers of extreme situations, he is a master of detail and of not yet discovered views. He has the eye of the connoisseur and the heart of a child. Waters are his love, mountains his longing, discovering the unknown world his passion, the world of eternal darkness - peace and calmness, people in nature and in the middle of life - dynamics.
Bogdan Kladnik is a poet of beauty and captive of aesthetic charm. He documents the microcosm and the macrocosm of nature and of man in it through his objective. He has obviously experienced too much knowledge in the vertical of mountains and waterfalls to remain just average.
Knowledge has its limits, beauty does not."

dr. Janez Marolt